Poetry
FOR THE
Love
of God

BOOK 1

B.J. NORWOOD

Poetry for the Love of God
Copyright © 2021 by B.J. Norwood. All rights reserved.

No part of this publication may be reproduced, stored in a retrieval system or transmitted in any way by any means, electronic, mechanical, photocopy, recording or otherwise without the prior permission of the author except as provided by USA copyright law.

This novel is a work of fiction. Names, descriptions, entities, and incidents included in the story are products of the author's imagination. Any resemblance to actual persons, events, and entities is entirely coincidental.

The opinions expressed by the author are not necessarily those of URLink Print and Media.

1603 Capitol Ave., Suite 310 Cheyenne, Wyoming USA 82001
1-888-980-6523 | admin@urlinkpublishing.com

URLink Print and Media is committed to excellence in the publishing industry.

Book design copyright © 2021 by URLink Print and Media. All rights reserved.

Published in the United States of America

Library of Congress Control Number: 2020925962
ISBN 978-1-64753-621-3 (Paperback)
ISBN 978-1-64753-622-0 (Digital)

19.05.20

Contents

He Gave Me Wings 1
How Am I to Know? 4
Finding Jesus 7
See and Seek 10
Selfish Side of Me 12
Something Missing 14
The Silent Night 18
Fret Not 21
Praise 23
Touch 25
Faith 27
Agony of Sins 29
Tomorrow 32
All Yours 34
Do a Good Deed 36
His Joy 38
It's the Pride 40
Slow Down 43
Stranger in the Mirror 45
This Time It's True 48
With You 52
I Hear You 54
One More Face 56
Fasting and Prayer 61
Merry Christmas 63
You and I 66
Confess 68
I Will Serve You 71
This Day 74
I Love You, Lord! 76
Who's to Blame? 78
Evil Winds 80
I'm Sorry, Lord 84
Caged within a Cage 86

He Gave Me Wings

In a land, of great peacefulness
is where I find myself.
It's as if I'm standing in the presence of God,
with his Spirit of love and no one else.

I'm showered by a blessing sun,
lending the warmth, of its calming rays.
My heart is greeted by a contentment,
that I desire for the rest of my days.

And there's a life-sustaining breeze,
gently kissing me on my face.
There's a beautiful flavor in my mouth.
It's the sweetness of God's grace.

I lie, without a worry, in the green grass,
that has now become my bed.
I have come to know no hunger,
while, by the brook of mercy, I lay my head.

Just as I'm about to close my eyes
and settle in to take my rest,
I guess it should be no surprise,
but I'm again met with a test.

For the grass has now turned to sand
as I arise to take another look.
The sun now burns like fire
and only rocks fill the brook.

From a distance, I see dust rising
and it comes from every direction.
If this be a storm in the brewing,
I have no shelter for my protection.

Oh look! It's my enemies from all ages,
each with a weapon of his choice.
They have anger in their eyes
and I hear death in every voice.

The enemies are come to destroy me,
but my heart knows no fear.
The world will not still my joy,
for the power of God has brought me here.

Closer and closer comes the foe,
but against them I do not lift a hand.
For I carry not sword nor shield,
how then am I able to stand.

Now they have approached me,
yet I have not a word to say.
Because the God of Heaven gave me wings,
so I spread them and fly away!

Yes, I was wounded by the enemy,
but mercy has shielded me from pain.
And though I smelled the fragrance of death,
she has gone and left no stain.

Now I fly the airs of tranquility.
I have no doubts and not a care.
For he made an oasis in the valley of death.
And I know God will always be there.

How Am I to Know

I know how I got here at first,
like everybody else through mother's womb.
But you say I can be born again
and all on this side of the tomb!

You say a group stood by the sea
and were able to walk across the seabed.
But then an army took chase
and the water receded and made them dead.

Once upon a time, way back when,
You say man's heart wasn't quite right.
And you say somehow it affected the weather,
so it rained for forty days and forty nights.

A man went out to kill his newborn son,
but ended up killing something like a goat.
Then another man stood by the water
and he got to see an ax that floats.

Three men were intentionally trapped in a fire
and none of them received even a little burn.
I consider myself a bright individual,
but it seems I have a lot yet to learn.

One man rides into town on an ass,
and another ass was able to speak.
How is one to know all these things?
So many answers do I seek.

Daniel hangs out with hungry lions
and it seem they are joined at the hip.
Then Ezekiel talks about a flying chariot,
who knew God cruised around in a spaceship!

A man lives for over nine hundred years
And his youth didn't come from a fountain.
And with an itty bitty amount of faith,
a person will be able to move a mountain.

This poor little old, tired, and weary lady,
she had been sick for so very long.
One day she touched a man's clothes
and poof! Twelve years of sorrow was gone.

As I grow old and somewhat feeble,
I find some of this remarkably clever.
For, you say, not only can I be born again,
but I can also somehow live forever!

So a man laid down his life for others!
What more could any man possible give.
You say he was dead for just about three days,
but you say that somehow he yet lives.

But exactly why am I here?
how should I live out each day?
Is there some type of guide to be found,
that would show me the right way?

You say the answers are at my fingertips,
to me that sounds so very absurd.
How am I to know all of these things?
maybe, just maybe, I should read his word!

Finding Jesus

Hello! Hello, cold and cruel world.
Is there anybody saved out there?
I'm just another poor lost soul.
Is there anyone that really cares?

I travel each day in total darkness.
My soul desires to end this void.
Can any of you please tell me
where I might go to find the Lord.

I need to have a clean heart.
I'm told he can renew my mind.
I need to find him at once,
for I feel I'm running out of time.

I'm in need of his holy redemption,
but help can I seem to find.
Can't you see without his forgiveness
I will surely be left behind.

I heard he would be returning soon.
And I don't want to be left out.
So I'm in great need for someone
to show me what being saved is all about.

So if there be any saved among you,
please stand up and let me know.
For if the righteous can't help me,
tell me whether [where] shall I go!

I went to search in the library
and only saw book on top of book.
I tried to find him on the Internet,
but Jesus is no place I look.

So I looked for Christ in the school,
but the governor said he was expelled.
Then I checked for him in the courtrooms,
but it was all to no avail.

I walked all of the popular streets,
but Jesus could not be found.
If Christians don't stand up,
the world is in for a big letdown.

I looked for Jesus in the congress,
but someone slipped me a note.
It said I couldn't find Jesus here,
for he doesn't get to vote.

Then it finally dawned on me,
the place my search could not avoid,
for the place I should definitely find Jesus,
must be the house of the Lord.

So I looked for Jesus in the chapel,
but was told he's out sick today.
You see the keepers are adulterers
and the prophet is gay.

Still I'm determined to find the Lord.
though where I may not know.
But my search would be made easier,
if the redeemed of the Lord would just say so!

See and Seek

See the sun up in the sky.
Seek to know the reason why.
See the waves of the ocean.
Seek the one that put them in motion.
See the grass that turns to feed.
Seek the one that made the seed.
See the moon shining at night.
Seek the one that is the light.
See the acorn that becomes the tree.
Seek him that caused it to be.
See the desert covered with sand.
Seek the one that has made the land.
See the mountain capped with snow.
Seek the one that made it so.

See the river and all it hath.
Seek the one that carved its path.
See the canyon and all its creatures.
Seek the one that gave it features.
See the rain as it's coming down.
Seek the one who gave it sound.
See the lightning that chills the soul.
Seek him that keeps it controlled.
See the stars that are so far away.
Seek the one who has caused them to stay.
See the winter that fades into spring.
Seek he who's in charge of everything.
See the birds as they fly away.
Seek Christ who's near you every day.

Selfish Side of Me

I'm blessed to have these four bedrooms.
But now two of them are free.
Storing a few old and wonderful memories
is their only real use left for me.

I saw people sleeping along the street
and I pretended they weren't even there.
So I let fear conquer my faith
and they never knew how much God even cares.

I've always wanted this mansion,
a treasure laid up unto myself.
But I only need a much smaller house,
then I could buy one for someone else.

God has truly been kind to me,
from walking to two cars and a truck.
You know! I could really look around
and share with someone down on their luck.

When shopping, I found three for the price of one.
Again God has shown me favor.
Maybe I should buy a little extra
and share with a poor friend or a neighbor.

Lord, here I am once again,
just enjoying all the comforts of home.
But if I'm dedicated to serving God,
then shouldn't I forsake my comfort zone.

Yes, we should enjoy blessings from God,
but maybe here's a little twist.
I'm here to serve this present age,
but who knows that I even exist.

If I seek to be a Good Samaritan,
then shouldn't I be on the move.
How much service can I render unto God
if I stay trapped within my own little groove.

I realize that God has granted me favor.
And it's a lot more than I really deserve.
Then why do I selfishly use his blessings
as an excuse not to serve.

Since God has given me my entire life,
don't I owe him a great portion of each day.
I could be a valuable tool for Christ,
if I could just get out of my own way.

Something Missing

Lord, you know for me times have been rough,
trying to raise a family on my own.
And going through each day can be tough,
when the only man you trust is gone.

You find someone to share your life
and at first beauty is all you see.
So you decide to become husband and wife,
thinking that's the way it will always be.

At the outset he was totally there,
in my heart he was the perfect man.
It was nice having someone to care,
But Satan came and changed the plan.

Years went and the kids came,
and we made for them a loving home.
For a season I felt so ashamed,
because the man I loved now is gone.

I didn't think our lives were so bad,
each day was filled with hugging and kissing.
But with all that we had,
I guess something was still missing.

He took very good care of us,
as a father, he was simply the best.
But now I work from dawn until dusk,
and the kids still have to settle for less.

He used to get up early in the morning
and he would go to work all day.
At night I would often see him yawning,
yet, with the kids, he took time to play.

On Saturday he was here at home,
taking care of little odds and ends.
Either he was bragging about the kids on the phone,
or outside showing them off to his friends.

Sundays were always very sweet,
for he always had something planned for us to do.
Like taking the family out to eat,
or maybe spending time at the zoo.

I remember wiping their little behind,
while he would clean the baby's nose.
For us joy was so easy to find.
It was fun just choosing baby clothes.

But now as I go from room to room,
It's me doing all the kissing.
Now the nights are shaded with gloom,
for as I turn I find there's something missing.

I still have memories of that awful day.
when he said there's something to talk about.
He said, "I just can't go on living this way
and I think it time I got out."

I remember being bombarded with pains and fears,
for somehow I couldn't seem to understand.
I tried so hard to hold back the tears,
But they were too much for my trembling hand.

He said, "Honey it's me, not you.
So don't go blaming yourself.
You did all I could expect you to do,
but something's missing and I need something else."

But he still seems to love his kids
and he manages to come by now and then.
Though I can't forgive him for what he did,
we somehow find a way to remain friends.

So I tell myself tat life goes on,
as I try to hold what's left in one piece.
My friends say to move on and be strong,
but they can't tell me when the pain will cease.

But then my kids came to me the other day
and said they want to talk and please listen.
They asked me to teach them how to pray.
then I realized that you Lord, were our something missing.

The Silent Night

Deep into the night and I'm all alone.
The silence is screaming into my ear.
Suddenly the silence became broken,
when out of nowhere a voice I hear.

It's a mighty calming voice,
that seems to carry no audio.
But I'm not at all frightened,
for it's a voice that I already know.

It's the voice of the redeemer,
so you know I don't mind.
For I promised to avail myself,
and he can call upon me at any time.

I inquired within as to his purpose.
Thinking it would be likes times before.
So I asked what he desired of me
and the Savior, from heaven, said MORE.

Have I not given you my all?!
What more do I have to give?
I have made up mind,
that you died for me and for you I live.

But I have not withheld my grace.
My kindness hath given you many pleasures.
Tell me, friend, where's your heart?
Where have you lain up your treasures?

But Lord! I've volunteered here
and I've served you over there.
I've given food unto the hungry
and showed the poor that you care.

I visited the sick
and prayed beside deathbeds.
I've tended unto your flock
and many of sheep have I fed.

I've carried your word by day
and sang unto you praises by night.
And though the battle seems hopeless,
still I stand in there and fight.

Your faithfulness goes not unnoticed.
Through my spirit, I've heard your cry.
Know in your heart that you yet live
because my mercy did not let you die.

I too have witnessed your past.
And indeed you have made a start.
But recall that which I commanded of you,
to love me with all of your mind, soul, body, and heart.

I have honored your sacrifice.
Your obedience is never to be wrong.
But service is not rooted in convenience.
Give unto me your comfort zone.

My people have perverted my word.
And evil abounds like never before.
In this time of great falling away,
It's from the faithful that I require more.

Continue to walk, therefore, in love,
but place nothing or no one before me.
For my blood alone has covered your sins
and only my truth will set you free.

So again I stand knocking,
again I stand at the door.
And when you have done all you know,
I still require a little bit more!

Fret Not

The future of our ailing society
can sometimes seems to be bleak.
But is there a real cause to worry,
or is my thinking just getting weak?

It seems that all around the world
Christians are becoming the target for the kill.
Every nation and every man has an agenda
and the quest for godliness is all uphill.

Prayer is all but kicked to the curve,
and unity is destined for defeat.
Personal desire is now the drum major
and righteousness has taken the backseat.

But stand fast and refuse to jump ship,
for God is still the driving force.
Jesus has taken the helm as the captain
and the Holy Spirit has plotted out the course.

God has laid out his chartered plan,
even before the time of our birth.
Then Jesus promised to be with us
even until the very end of the earth.

When the news has become frightening
and things don't look as they should,
fret not, for God makes things work together
and come into focus just for our good.

Praise

Let God have your praise
in any way you can give.
And he is always close to you,
for in his praise is where he lives.

Praise ye the Lord for always,
be it midday or at midnight.
Praise him with all honesty
and feel your burdens get light.

Praise God throughout the year,
for he is worthy in every season.
Praise him in good and bad times,
then praise Jesus without a reason.

Praise God wherever you may be
and watch his Holy Spirit appear.
Praise Jesus with a sincere heart,
then you will know he's near.

Praise God in the middle of your storm
and watch as all of that worry fades.
Praise him both young and old,
for his grace covers all decades.

Praise God for giving us salvation,
through the blood that covers our shame.
Praise God for his redeeming Son
and the power of his holy name.

Touch

Touch your heart with a song.
Touch God's heart with a praise.
Touch the life of a struggling mother,
by helping her child to be raised.

Touch the heart of your friend.
Then touch the heart of a stranger.
Touch the mind of a neighbor's son,
to help keep him out of danger.

Touch the heart of the lonely.
Tell them they are not alone.
Touch the ills of the weak
and help them to become strong.

Touch the ego of the exalted.
Then touch the hand of the downtrodden.
Touch the path of the unrighteous,
that God's purpose be not forgotten.

Touch the eyes of the blind,
that by faith they might see.
Touch the minds of the captive,
that by grace they might be free.

Touch the air of confusion,
that there may be peace.
Touch the plight of the homeless,
that they may have increase.

Touch the spirit of the righteous,
that he be not tempted to stray.
Touch the minds of the doubtful,
that they kneel with you and pray.

Touch a sinner with scriptures.
And pray that he comes out of the mud.
Pray that he may see the light
and become washed in the Holy Blood.

So reach out and touch someone.
Because, unknowingly, it can do so much.
Remember that twelve years of bad blood
was once healed because of a simple touch.

Faith

FAITH is a bridge
that crosses a sea of doubt.
When drowning in a lake of sin,
it is faith that pulls you out.

FAITH is like a muscle.
Use it and it gets stronger.
If you don't use it,
you don't have it much longer.

FAITH is an inward light
that has an outward glow.
It brightens as times get darker
and it seeks to let God show.

FAITH is like a repair kit,
it can rebuild a man's heart.
Faith is like a passport,
lets you into the presence of God.

FAITH is like the rising sun,
a constant source of power.
Faith is like Niagara Falls,
a continuing cleansing shower.

FAITH is extremely sustaining,
like a never-ending well.
Faith is like a detour sign,
that helps to bypass the gates of hell.

FAITH is, within itself, a seed,
from which many things grow.
And the number of fruits it bears
is more than we could ever know.

Agony of Sins

Save Thy servant, oh Lord!
And why have I done this?
I thought I was free from sin.
Tell me what did I miss!

My heart seeks to spread your joy,
while my deeds only begat more pain.
Forgiveness hides from thee my transgressions,
but memory recaptures the stain.

Why have I done this evil deed?
Why have I purchased this fate?
Why do I seek to please the flesh?
And become that which I hate!

How can I sit in my sins
if I'm to walk in your name?
How can the father love the child
that brings him so much shame?

I'm convinced that I've done this,
though it never crossed my mind.
My heart is padded now by guilt
because the "why" I cannot find.

Troubles have transcended my youth
and seek to haunt me of old.
Create in me a clean heart, oh Lord,
and return your joy unto my soul.

Hear my plea for Mercy, oh Lord,
There's no other help that I know.
When thou has hidden thy face,
there is no other place I can go.

How could I walk not in your way?
when I've come to know your will.
But my members are flooded with evil,
seeking to quench and to kill.

I subject myself unto your law,
then I find that there are two.
For flesh seeks after the flesh,
but my mind is stayed on you!

If I desire to be in your glory,
then I must somehow find the way.
I find I must die not only once,
but I must die each and every day.

If I have thrown this rock,
why have I hidden my hand?
How am I to conquer this demon,
unless I first come to understand!

How can I enter into thy kingdom?
How can I behold thy face?
Unless you show unto me your mercy
and shower me with your grace!

Tomorrow

Tomorrow awaits as she holds her course.
Ready in due time to give her piercing light.
She bears no shame and holds no remorse,
   As she reveals the secrets of the night.

Tomorrow comes to us as no surprise,
   For as a warning she sends the dawn.
   But when her beams greet our eyes,
Who shall be faultless or who shall be scorned.

Tomorrow has manufactured for us a reality,
   From what was, yesterday, only dreams.
   And what we think today will always be,
   Tomorrow is ripping apart at the seams.

Yesterday has trampled, leaving his miserable stain.
And today is causing many of us to cry.
But tomorrow brings an end to our pain,
For Jesus has promised to wipe us dry.

Today when I don't quite understand,
Yesterday tends to share a little light.
But if we let Jesus hold our hand,
Our tomorrows will always be bright.

Tomorrow transforms the future into the present,
While folding our today into the past.
So many things we do are good and pleasant,
But only what's done for Christ will last.

All Yours

I stand in thy presence a pardoned soul.
All my sins have been confessed.
I come carrying no great need,
for thou art faithful and I am blessed.

From my childhood You have been near,
always my strong post to lean on.
You turned my sorrows into joy
and my enemies into stepping stones.

When the wicked have surrounded me
and I could see evilness in their faces,
your mercy gave unto me wings,
that I may find peace in your high places.

Death had placed grips on my soul,
but You said that I should live.
For all the wonders thou have done,
there must be something that I can give.

So I give unto You my mind, oh Lord,
that it is forever stayed on thee.
Then I'll seek new ways to serve you,
while living within your perfect peace!

I give unto You my voice
and ask you for the words to say.
Then I give to You my eyes.
Help me show someone your way.

I give unto Thee my heart
and all that may lie there within.
I pray that You will sanctify it
and teach me how to be your friend.

I offer unto You my soul,
that it may be yours to keep.
Bath it with your joy, dear Lord,
that I may awake before I sleep.

I offer unto You this bag of bones
and I'll do all that I can do.
But when they cast eyes upon me,
let them cast their minds on You.

So fill me with their Holy Spirit.
Let my heart burn with the fire!
Make me into a faithful servant
and use me as You desire!

Do a Good Deed

So You are off and on your way.
Please take time to plant a seed.
You are blessed to see another day.
Please take time to do a good deed.

Sometimes it doesn't take a whole lot
to show what's inside of You.
Just share a little of what you got
and see how much good it can do.

Let love suffer no blindness,
regardless of the time or the season.
Because truth about our kindness
is that it requires no special time or reason.

So go ahead and hug a child,
even if it's not your own.
And give away a comforting smile,
even if to someone that's fully grown.

Go on and sow your seed.
Who knows exactly how it will grow.
Desire often to do a good deed
and one may just knock on your door.

Keep your head up and mind your step,
even when in the checkout line.
If needed, offer a little help,
it may be an angel that You stand behind.

Yes! I've heard bad things that were said,
but you can help others even in the rain.
You may even be a little afraid,
but people need help just the same.

I don't claim to know exactly how God feels,
but I do know what his word say.
Since he and his love are for real,
shouldn't we share them every day!

See that man holding up that sign.
It's either true or it's a lie.
But that worry is not really mine,
because for all I do, Jesus is the "why."

Some things they won't appreciate
and you're with nothing to say.
But never in life should you hesitate
to do a good deed anyway.

His Joy

Traveling down the roads of life,
troubles sometimes take its toll.
Burdens tends to drown my heart,
then she comes and flood my soul.

Standing all alone in a crowd,
at times I feel so out of place.
Then she comes to ease my mind
and puts a smile back on my face.

When I get that sinking feeling
and it seems hard to carry on,
she comes, by the Spirit of God,
bringing me the strength to make me strong.

Look! Here she comes again,
and just when I need her most.
She leads me into a time of prayer
until I'm revived by the Holy Ghost.

I seemingly fight this battle by myself,
but she tells me I'm not alone.
Then she takes the fear from my heart
and replaces it with a song.

She has a way of growing faith,
while transforming hearts of stone.
She usually accompanies his righteousness,
but offers no pleasure in doing wrong.

She causes us to seek out the Lord
and his praises to employ.
One of God's greatest gifts,
after the Son and Spirit, is his joy.

It's the Pride

What type of thing can this be?
that tells me I'm better than You.
Even when the word of God
tells me that it's just not true.

When I stop to look at You,
it tells me I'm in a better place.
But it never gives me a warning
when I'm about to fall on my face.

It makes me boast of being right,
sometimes even when I know I'm wrong.
It tells me I need help from no man
and that I made it here on my own.

It convinces me that I'm special,
with merit in all that I do.
It says you should all but worship me,
while I make effort to tolerate you.

Take a look at all the things I have.
And cherish the works of my past.
Erect unto me images of my likeness,
that memories of my deeds will last.

It's telling me who can be my friend,
who has the same lineage as me.
It told me how I should speak.
Now it tells me how I should see.

Don't associate with that kind.
They are not of the same class.
It gave me a heart made of stone
and a house made of glass.

It tells me to walk among the elite
and not condescend to men of low estate.
Never mind the plight of the peasants,
leave them to rot in their own fate.

It comes to bring me self-pleasures,
just look at the plaques along the wall.
It falsifies the value of my worth
and then goes just before I fall.

It can destroy unity of a family.
even to the point where no one will speak.
I can feel it as it grows stronger,
but failing to see how it makes me weak.

It has a bloodline of its own,
jealousy and envy are its kin.
Together or alone, each one is deadly,
walking down the path of sin.

Slow Down

I really think you should slow down a bit.
You might be moving a little too fast.
You know the faster you go,
the sooner you run out of gas.

Just leave a little earlier
and choose a slower pace.
You can take in more of the sights
and keep the wind out of your face.

When you go slow enough,
you can offer someone else a ride.
And when you release the love,
you increase the joy inside.

Slow down a little bit more
and remember the sign you just read.
It tells you the speed considered safe,
but it can't tell you all the dangers that lie ahead.

Take a little time and you will see
the bumps and curves of the road.
Don't forget that speed has a way
of sending troubles into overload.

Time is not under your control.
It's something you can never save.
I know you want things done right now,
but remember God is not your microwave.

A person should always take time out
to praise God for all he or she hath.
Then move just slow enough
for God to direct their path.

It's time to slow down now.
For God has put up his stop sign.
Let his Spirit go and clear the danger
and he will give you peace of mind.

God has placed his signs along the road.
But you must take the time to see.
He says to take your foot off the pedal
and keep your mind stayed on thee.

God is trying to speak to you,
but velocity is killing the sound.
You'll hear his voice more clearly,
if you would just slow down!

Stranger in the Mirror

When I look into the mirror,
There's a stranger that I see.
Though he has captured all of my features,
but he really looks nothing like me.

He's standing there just looking at me,
as though he thinks we maybe friends.
I may have met him in my past,
but looks like he's full of sin.

He has the markings of a thief
and I'll wager that he has fornicated.
He seems to be no friend of the peace.
How much trouble has he instigated?

I've seen his kind around here before,
you know, the egotistic type.
He's God's gift to all the world,
that is if you believe all of his hype.

He looks like a crime in progress,
just out looking for a place.
He carries wickedness in his heart
and a warming smile on his face.

He wears a disguise to hide the evil,
a lot of attraction with very little class.
He doesn't have much of a future,
this monster of a distant past.

I'm glad to have received God's grace.
It's a great blessing to be set free.
He has washed me in his redeeming blood
and saved me from this stranger I see.

I recognize your evil ways,
as you try to change my mind.
But I will refuse all communion with you
and vow to leave you far, far behind.

He invites me to come over,
but I just can't seem to make the time.
His paths would all lead me into trouble,
and he's not the forgiven kind.

He takes pride in the way he cheats,
living a life that's full of tricks.
He's quick to give you his word,
but he can't seem to make it stick.

He wants to talk about good times
and the misdeeds of his childhood.
But I see his dreams and aspirations
seem all to lead into no good.

This stranger, that is in my mirror,
is worthy only of total condemnation.
The mirror suggests that we look the same,
but the mirror does not reflect my salvation.

This Time It's True

A new baby entered into the world.
And I had no idea what life was about.
But by the time I reached age five,
I thought I had it all figured out.

Then one day I started to go to school,
and my life got so very exciting.
Then this revelation soon came,
Mama and Santa has the same handwriting.

Tomorrow we'll find presents beneath the tree.
And the whole day will be filled with fun.
But how can he come down the chimney,
when my house doesn't even have one!

A furry-faced man baring gifts,
it all sounds so well and good.
But carrying goodies and fresh venison,
he wouldn't last long in my neighborhood.

However, a man will come bearing gifts by night,
he promised eternal life for me and for you.
He has purchased for us our salvation
and this time it's true!

Tonight is time for a huge celebration.
I've waited all year for New Year's Eve!
The new year is never going to go right,
unless we start it with ham hocks and black-eyed peas!

I don't know if the groundhog even has a shadow,
but I know it doesn't change the season.
So many people have fallen in love,
but a baby-sized man, with arrows, was never the reason.

On one day, the Lord died,
but he rose again in just about three.
He came to save those that would be lost.
and he came to set the captive free.

Some people chuckle at this truth,
a soured heart somehow finds it funny.
But is it so hard to believe in Christ,
or that an egg comes from a bunny!

So please stop and take this to heart,
regardless of how you may presently feel.
Because this time it is so very true,
the Father, Son, and Holy Spirit are all so real.

Through the years, I faced so many trials and troubles,
but, by faith, I always made it over.
My victories were never to be determined,
by the number of leaves on a clover.

I was never taken by the bogeyman,
but what fear had bound faith has set loose.
And no little winged lady ever entered my room
to exchange money for a dislodged tooth.

No super human hero ever came to my rescue,
in my times of peril or despair.
But my relief always seems to come,
by turning my face to the ground and my heart to the air.

So just move on all ye masked and marveled men.
To thee I bid a fond and final farewell.
For there is a God that I must uphold
and there's a truth that I must tell.

Remember that no matter where you are,
nor what other people may say or do,
You have a super savior in Jesus
and this time it's true!

With You

With you each day becomes an adventure
And the nights are filled with pleasures.
The troubles become the challenges
And the simple becomes the treasures.

With you, loneliness has become a myth
And the storm is just a shower.
Your touch becomes my peace
And your words become my power.

With you a heart becomes a temple
And happiness aides in a song.
Your faithfulness becomes my staff
And the weak becomes the strong.

With you giving becomes the norm
And the famished becomes the fed.
The meek becomes the mighty
And the mighty becomes the led.

With you the lost finds the path
And the ostracized has a friend.
The weary acquires lasting comfort
And hatred meets its end.

With you peace comes within a smile
And the old becomes the new.
The perished receives immortality
And I come alive with you.

I Hear You

So much time and so far away,
Yet, I still hear your voice.
But with all of this shame, what do I say,
And how do I make the right choice?

You say you still love me,
And in my heart I know it's true.
But at times I ask how can that be,
After all I've put you through.

You promised to always hold my hand
And I promised to always lift your name.
But I let go when I thought I couldn't stand
And got washed into this pool of shame.

This old feeling I keep trying to shake,
But Lord the pain is much too deep.
I pray that somehow I will awake
Before my soul falls to sleep.

Yes, I know you are still there,
Because I still hear you calling.
And Lord it's not that I don't care,
But as I keep trying I keep falling.

So I ask, Lord, for your help.
And for your Spirit, so holy and so true.
May he guide me through each and every step.
And I'll know I can make it through.

May he forever walk with me
And daily wash me through and through.
That your word is all I see
And your will for me may come true.

Yes! I hear you, Lord,
And finally I'm on my way.
So please fill me with thy Spirit
And, Lord, hear me when I pray.

One More Face

Here is the tale of war,
no winners when everybody lose [loses].
Lessened is your chance at redemption,
when war is what you choose.

War is just a foul and deadly game,
in which no one can ever win.
Of course there will be plenty of death.
Tell me, what's the wages of sin.

At another time and another place,
and you are my very close friend.
But when face-to-face on the battlefield,
one life has to come to an end.

That which I cherish the most,
I must take from someone else.
How do I begin to ask God for forgiveness?
when I know I'll never forgive myself.

You finished at the top of the class.
You were such a bright young man.
Now I collect your body parts
and try to brush away the sand.

How are we ever to survive this?
The season is so dreadfully hot.
Oh, excuse me for a moment,
while I take aim for another shot.

So where are you from, my friend?
And tell me where's your head!
Why do I bother to talk to you,
obviously you are already dead.

I see by that final look on your face,
this was not your finest day.
Here's wishing the soul a happy journey,
as I watch another life slip away.

Here I see good men die
and in no way is that considered cool.
This is so far from that love and stuff
that we talked about back in Sunday school.

Heck, the dead are the lucky ones,
they don't bare the loss of friends.
For them this hell is over,
but for some it never ends.

And what about ALL of those faces.
They creep into your sleep.
They make it hard for me to breathe
and destroys my desire to eat.

The streaming faces of condemnation
are torturing me with silent pain.
Innocent faces reflecting my guilt,
are altering the functions of my brain.

I see faces of men bleeding out.
Bubbles appear as they gasp for air.
Faces of a son crying for his dad,
saying he's gone and it's just not fair.

I see my mother's smiling face,
says do what you want done unto you.
I see the face of my father,
to love God you must love man too!

I see faces of my comrades,
as families gather to say good-bye.
I see faces of mothers weeping,
and I can hear the children cry.

As the years come and years go,
nightmares, background get rearranged.
The faces seem to age with time,
but their message has not changed.

Why have you come to our land?
Why have you brought so much pain?
All our lives are touched by this evil
and nothing will ever be the same.

At home they call me a hero,
but I find no reason to cheer.
Life has now caused me to question,
just why am I still here!

People that I deemed greater than I,
have come to meet a bitter end.
Why is it that I must destroy a man?
when I'd rather make him a friend.

How am I to escape this madness?
Do I seek redemption from above?
Considering all the evil that I've done,
have I bypassed the limits of God's love.

So if I'm to have no place with thee,
believe me I will truly understand.
But I desire to see just one more face,
the face of he who has made man!

Fasting and Prayer

Time spent in fasting and prayer
gives more food unto the soul.
For this wallowing in our sins
sure can quickly get old.

Flesh and spirit are always at war.
The one fed the most will be stronger.
The muscles that you use properly
will tend to last you longer.

More than just a mere recommendation,
it's a valuable way to spend your time.
Not only will it clear up your vision,
but it frees and strengthens your mind.

You feel your faith as it starts to grow,
while putting your heart into a groove.
It gives you favor with the Lord
and confidence to say, "Move, mountain, move!"

It put into perspective things you hear
and adds a boldness unto what you say.
You no longer sweat the small things,
for just like mountains, they get out of your way.

You may have felt a little down,
but you'll be in a higher place when done.
You'll be a little further from the world,
but a lot closer to the Son.

You put yourself into the driver's seat.
And things will start to go your way.
God will cause so much good to come
when you stop to fast and pray.

Merry Christmas

Merry Christmas
a child is borne.
Merry Christmas
let not his name be scorned.
Merry Christmas
come let us recall his birth.
Merry Christmas
where's my peace on earth?
Merry Christmas
Let us seize the day.
Merry Christmas
For whom shall I pray?
Merry Christmas
look at where they sleep.
Merry Christmas
let's take one off the street.
Merry Christmas
each face is adorned with a smile.
Merry Christmas
let's make one less needed child.
Merry Christmas
come, let us not hesitate.

Merry Christmas
condescend to men of low estate.
Merry Christmas
give the name of Christ a lift.
Merry Christmas
let your service be your gift.
Merry Christmas
with our souls, let us not roll the dice.
Merry Christmas
be a living sacrifice.
Merry Christmas
take a glance at the stars above.
Merry Christmas
Let us shine forth his love.
Merry Christmas
let those joy bells ring!
Merry Christmas
give praises unto our king.
Merry Christmas
set the white doves free.

Merry Christmas
who's in need of me.
Merry Christmas
may this joy have no end.
Merry Christmas
who's in need of a true friend?
Merry Christmas
I must give someone a call.
Merry Christmas
did I give God my all?
Merry Christmas
welcome, family and friends, into our home.
Merry Christmas
God is still watching from his throne.
Merry Christmas
not much more to say.
Merry Christmas
Let this be every day!

You and I

I tell them about your offer of salvation,
but they just don't seem to hear.
You warned them of impending condemnation,
but the foolish knows not fear.

I try to guide them through utter confusion,
to lessen their grief and strife.
You promised that at death's conclusion,
we would gain an everlasting life.

I tell them of your endless love,
that they may have peace throughout the land.
You sent your Spirit from above,
that we may know your helping hand.

I grant aid unto the weak,
and try to guide them along.
You have displayed power when you speak,
and thy grace has made them strong.

I must not travel this road alone,
for at times I slip and fall.
You made me mightier than the army of Rome,
that through you I may conquer all.

I see the seeds of the wicked grow,
the wheat and tares are in cohabitation.
You advised me to just let it go,
for You are the master of separation.

I tend to sit and weep sometimes,
for those that are dear to me,
You have wept for all of mankind,
and showed mercy for those who wouldn't see.

I sometimes get a sense of danger,
especially when in the midst of the unknown.
You gave your life for strangers
and then you made them your very own.

I sometimes think only of little ole me
and try to stay just shy of the grave.
You gave up your life to make me free
and that the whole world might be saved.

So I bow now to ask this favor,
that I may be more faithful and true.
That you make me over, oh blessed Savior,
and this time make me more like You.

Confess

Hey friend! Do you have a moment?
Let's sit and talk for a while.
I see there's sorrow in your heart
and you seem to have lost your smile.

Don't carry that problem around too long.
It can cause you to have a big mess.
I'm willing to share your burden,
if you are just willing to confess.

So just lay it all out on me.
Chances are I've already been there.
Even if I don't have all of the answers,
at least you'll know that I really care.

So just let your heart be free.
Don't be hindered by fear or shame.
For we both are trying to pay homage
and carry on in Jesus name.

Sometimes you may have my answer
and maybe sometimes I know what's best.
But God tends to help us much faster,
when we repent and confess.

We, sometimes, think it makes us strong
to just keep it all locked up inside.
But we bring so much sickness our way,
by clinging to our foolish pride.

Satan tends to lead us into the path of sin.
Then uses that sin to create a seed of doubt.
Then other types of wickedness start to grow,
because we didn't let the first one out.

You know there must be a reason,
God says to confess our sins one to the other.
Because the answers that we may seek,
he has already given to another.

The veins carry blood throughout the body.
Likewise, are we to carry God's love.
Our strength may lie within each other,
but it still comes from God up above.

So don't cause a spiritual blood clot.
Let the blood of love freely flow.
What affects you harms us all,
so please just confess and let it go.

Put your body and mind at ease.
There's no need to harbor that load of stress.
The only sins that are not forgiven,
are those we care not to confess.

Confession may cause some to take a second look.
But fear not, for you standing in God's name.
Because forgiveness has a cleansing way
of keeping our place, in God, just the same.

Without fear let's talk to each other
and then seek the Lord in prayer.
For wherever two or three gather in his name,
he has promised to meet us there.

We all travel this maze called life.
Only through Jesus do we have it made.
And through the power of our confessions,
his grace is rushed unto our aid.

We all sought to reach his glory,
but fell a little short at best.
Jesus awaits us with his restoration,
if only we would turn to him and confess.

I Will Serve You

Yes, I'm going to serve you, Lord.
I'm now determined to give you my all.
I've seen the sign and heard the whispers.
And now I will heed your call.

I understand it's not always easy
And not every day is sunny or nice.
But I have fully examined the cost
And I'm willing to pay the price.

Yes, some friends will laugh at me
And others will quietly fade away.
Some may attempt to discourage me,
But I will not be swayed by what they say.

No longer will be a member of the in crowd.
And at times I might find myself all alone.
But with Jesus as master of my soul,
How can I possibly go wrong?

All of those favorite places I used to go,
They seem so strange to me now.
And the crazy things I used to do
Aren't quite as much fun somehow.

Yes, I will serve you, my Lord,
For I know your burden is light.
And though troubles seem to keep on coming,
I know you will make everything all right.

So I give my heart to you, dear Lord,
While I praise you for your deed.
For you came and gave your life for me.
Then you left behind what you knew I would need.

So I'll follow in your way, my Lord.
And persuade others to do the same.
Though I be cut by the sword of ridicule,
I'll hold to the faith and not be ashamed.

Forever will I lift my soul to you, sweet Lord,
Stopping not even for a season.
Because, in your joy, I'll find my strength
And in you, oh Lord, I find my reason.

Family doesn't always understand me, Lord.
And at times they may let me down.
But you conquered death just for your friends
And no greater love could ever be found.

A lot of things have changed.
And I realize it's all for the best.
For my mind bathes in your peace now.
And my soul has come to know rest.

This Day

This day, one I've not seen before,
is another page in my human story.
I will sing his praises as I go
and give Jesus all the glory.

In his Spirit will I choose to pray,
in a tongue even I don't understand.
I will aid others while on my way
and to the needy I will lend a hand.

This day, in the Spirit, I will walk
and let God take control of my life.
If, at all, I'm able to talk,
I will tell of the wonders of Christ.

I'll let You know that I have no powers,
for unto Christ, God has given it all.
But just as the rain comes in showers,
so does he let his Spirit fall.

This day as I watch the heathen rage,
my faith and my light will not be hid.
My desire for his favor will not be waved,
even if I must suffer as Christ did!

I will stand up for what is right,
even if I must stand all alone.
In his name, I'll stay in this fight,
until he has called me home.

In this day, they say prayer is wrong
and everything gay appears to be right.
But I will grab Jesus and just hold on.
And I choose to walk in his light!

I will not let acceptance cause me to sway,
nor let popularity be my guide.
For though his truth turns some away,
I know Jesus is standing by my side.

This day, even more than in time past,
God is calling us to stand true.
We sit and let evil spread so fast,
while his light be hidden within me and you!

This day I will shine forth his light.
All who have eyes let them see.
For just as a thief in the night,
he will come for those whom he has set free!

I Love You, Lord

Lord, with all of my heart, I love You.
My love is greater than before.
When I think of all you've done,
Lord, I desire to love you more!

I will love You in times of plenty.
I'll love You when I have needs.
I want to love You with my words
and love You with my deeds.

I desire to love You when I'm all alone.
and I'll love You when in a crowd.
Let me love You beneath my breath,
and I promise to love You out loud.

I will love thee in the morning
and keep loving You through the night.
I love You when things are going wrong
and I love You when they are going right.

I'll love You with my voice,
all of your praises I will employ.
I love You with all of my soul,
for thou art my strength and my joy.

I will love You in sweet surrender
and to thee I'll raise my hands.
I will love thee with all my mind,
that Satan has no place to stand.

Let me love You with my body.
I surrender from head to toe.
And when I've loved You with all that I have,
Lord, I want to love you even more.

Who's to Blame

Today I stopped to take a look around,
just to see what was out there.
I saw that society's pants are falling down
and no one even seems to care.

I find that Jesus must be hurt,
by the dishonor brought upon his name.
So I decided to do a little research,
to try and see just who I should blame.

I sought to blame the preacher,
but he shouldn't have to stand alone.
So I tried to blame the teacher,
but who's teaching them at home?

I blamed the policeman carrying a loaded gun.
But he comes after you have gone astray.
Then I guess his job is all done
when he carries you in and lock you away.

I blamed the leaders that don't seem to lead.
I wonder when they will do their part.
But did they cause this social nosebleed,
when you can't legislate a man's heart.

Then I tried to blame the father,
too many kids wearing a maiden name.
But did anyone even bother
to give him the reason to change?

So I tried to blame the child
and wonder why he has gone astray.
We say he seems to have gone wild,
but who was there to show him the way?

We must not lose this fight!
And we must employ all of our labor.
If one puts a thousand and two ten thousands to flight,
then aren't the odds in our favor!

I blamed the curriculum that teaches evolution,
while saying prayer is not cool.
But this didn't start the spiritual revolution,
for which of us was saved by public school.

Search after search and this I find,
as a possible cause to this shame,
that when it comes to the bottom line,
maybe you and I are to blame.

Evil Winds

Quickly, take shelter in God's word,
for evil winds inhabit the land.
They blow debris into the eyes of the believers
and bring destruction unto the heart of man.

They have blown evil into high places
and blew prayer right out of our schools.
They have turned the scared into the ungodly
and turn wise men into fools.

They blew into the hearts of families
and ripped their fibers apart.
They caused shame to stand behind the altar
and brought death into the house of God.

They blew out the candle of righteousness.
And day is hidden within the night.
But if the church is to be silenced,
who will shine forth the light?

Truth is tilted and peace is smitten,
all in the name of what's right.
The people of God relinquish their commitment
without even putting up a fight.

Blown away is complete surrender
and contentment has soaked the ground.
The Spirit cries out for faithfulness,
but no one hears the sound.

Prejudice blew into the chambers
and the snake has cut off his head.
Unity has been blown away
and hope for prosperity is dead.

A great wind fell upon the mighty house
and there's no milk without the cow.
"One Nation Under God," tell us
who do you follow now?

Governments are blown into a halt,
by the winds of indecision,
And the people of God are slaughtered,
all in the name of religion.

Discontent blew across the Promised Land.
And distrust seeks to gain control.
Confusion has scattered her people
and dimmed the light of the soul.

Unbelief has roared through the valley.
Evil has now been given power.
The winds have torn off the roof
and now comes the shower.

With the wind, has gone the innocence.
Hear the hearts of the children cry.
For the bad has now become the good
and no one can tell them why.

The winds of fornication rumbles,
the wind of infidelity has sounded her horn.
Covetousness has infected the neighborhood,
and so many families have been torn.

The wind of greed released her fury
and has caused the people to hurry.
The wind of fear has toppled the heart
and caused the people to worry.

The wind, of looking back, made a turnaround,
the mountain of blindness is at fault.
Man, again, has become lover of himself
and obedience is now a pillar of salt.

There once stood spiritual boldness,
but the wind of doubt blew fear on top.
The winds of hatred is getting stronger.
Who knows when it will stop.

It has rained down deception
upon all but the very elect.
For those that the Lord has chosen,
the Holy Spirit vows to protect.

I sought the Lord for shelter
that I may run and hide.
He gave me strength to face the wind
and placed my refuge on the inside.

Those in Christ must face the winds,
regardless of what it may cost.
We must help to repair the broken
and share salvation with the lost.

Stand fast, oh children of God,
and be ye not deceived.
For what is now a mighty hurricane,
God will turn into a gentle breeze.

I'm Sorry, Lord

Lord, in shame I bow before you,
A soul attired in sin.
I've done what Satan said to do
And had desires of doing it again.

I sinned not by accident but by choice,
A heart subject to steal or fornicate.
And when Satan wanted a lying voice,
I was there willing to cooperate.

Desiring within to do thy will,
Yet giving in easily to do what's wrong.
Knowing that if I just keep still,
Thou would gladly make me strong.

Overlooking the commitment of confession
And not seeming to care.
I'm overwhelmed with an abundance of transgression
And sickened with a lack of prayer.

Just as the honeysuckle vine,
Smelling sweet and running wild.
Foolishly wasting your valuable time
And too embarrassed to be your child.

Forsaking years of Sunday school lessons,
To live a life of fruitless disgrace.
Taking for granted all of your blessings
And giving you a slap in the face.

I'm not worthy even to die,
But you saw fit that I should live.
You care for me without a why.
I'm sorry, Lord, please forgive.

Caged within a Cage

Here, standing in sin, am I.
Trapped like bird within a cage.
And though I hold my head up high,
I can not escape the terror of this rage.

It is I that I mostly mistreat
I'm guilty with or without the proof.
I tread on self-pity beneath my feet
and self-hate has become my roof.

Was I born to suffer this fate?
Why do I answer when sin calls?
If only I could breach the gate,
I could stop trying to climb the walls.

How am I to ever win this fight,
when the fight is within me?
In my members, I find no light.
How then shall I ever be free?

This path I did not choose.
It was predestined before my time.
How can I help but lose,
if I'm sentenced before the crime.

By the transgression of one am I cast down,
dislodged from the garden of grace.
Even if the chief angel came around,
he could not move me from this fate.

But I hear the mighty voice
of one who is watching over me.
His mercy is giving me a choice,
that I may be set free.

Though to sin the body be enslaved,
I'm free in my spirit and mind.
From the law of sin I'm saved,
because a new law in me I find.

He has brought peace to calm the rage,
of a soul not subjected to Satan's kill.
My cage is within a larger cage,
as I now tarry within God's will.

To forgo the impending disaster
and to return unto the holy grace,
I have chosen a forgiving master
to lead me into a higher place.

I await my master's return,
when he will transform the old.
He will give me what I have not earned,
a body befitted for the soul.

Then all shackles will be broken
and all sin will cease to be.
He will fulfill all that he has spoken
and we shall forever be free.

www.ingramcontent.com/pod-product-compliance
Lightning Source LLC
LaVergne TN
LVHW011732060526
838200LV00051B/3148